# HOW TO DRAW SUPER VILLAINS

Illustrated by **Jael**

Copyright © 1994 Kidsbooks Inc.
3535 West Peterson Avenue
Chicago, IL 60659

Manufactured in the United States of America

# INTRODUCTION

This book will show you how to draw lots of different supervillains. Some are more difficult than others, but if you follow along, step-by-step, you'll soon be able to draw any supervillain you wish.

## SUPPLIES

NUMBER 2 PENCILS
SOFT ERASER
DRAWING PAD

FELT-TIP PEN
COLORED PENCILS, MARKERS,
OR CRAYONS

Each figure in this book begins with a **line or stick figure**. This establishes the movement of the supervillain. Then, different kinds of **oval** shapes are added over the line figure to round out the basic sections of the body. Other shapes will also be used.

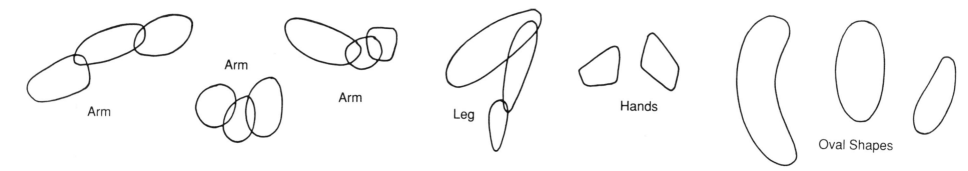

Arm

Arm

Arm

Leg

Hands

Oval Shapes

The basic shapes usually overlap when forming the arms and legs.

The first two steps create a **solid foundation** of the figure — much like a builder who must first construct a foundation before building the rest of the house. Next comes the fun part — creating the muscles, face, clothing, armor and weapons, and adding all the details and finishing touches.

## HELPFUL HINTS:

1. Following the first two steps carefully will make the final steps easier.
2. **Always keep your pencil lines light and soft**. These "guidelines" will be easier to erase when you no longer need them.
3. Don't be afraid to erase. It usually takes lots of drawing and erasing before you will be satisfied with the way your supervillain looks.

4. Add details and all the finishing touches **after** you have blended and refined all the shapes and your figure is complete.
5. You can check a pose by using yourself as a model. Just stand in front of a full-length mirror.
6. Remember: Practice Makes Perfect. Don't be discouraged if you can't get the "hang of it" right away. Just keep drawing and erasing until you do.

# HOW TO START

1. Begin by drawing a stick figure like the one on this page. This will help you make the figure move in the right direction. The action and movement of a figure is called **gesture.**
2. Add the oval shapes to the stick figure. Note that many of these ovals are not "perfect." These are the basic guidelines that form the body and create the foundation.

## *REMEMBER TO KEEP YOUR LINES LIGHTLY DRAWN*

### Foreshortening
Supervillains are shown in dramatic poses that include foreshortening. To understand this better, stand in front of a mirror and point to yourself with one arm. See how short your arm appears? Then hold your other arm straight out to your side. Now you can see your arm's normal length. An artist learns to draw things as the eye sees them, not as they really are. This gives the figure a realistic, 3-dimensional appearance.

3. Carefully draw the body muscles **within** the oval guidelines. The dotted lines show what can be erased as you go along. When you are satisfied with your drawing, erase the guidelines, including the stick figure.
4. Add facial features, hair, clothing, and all the other details and finishing touches to complete your supervillain drawing. Color your finished supervillains with your favorite colors or, for more dramatic effect, outline them with a thick, black marker.

Elsewhere in this book you will find illustrations of supervillain weapons. These are just **examples** of things you can add to a finished picture. Use your **imagination** and create different objects and backgrounds to enhance your supervillain drawings.
   When you have drawn some or all of the characters in this book, and are comfortable with the drawing technique, start creating your own supervillains.
   Most of all, **HAVE FUN!**

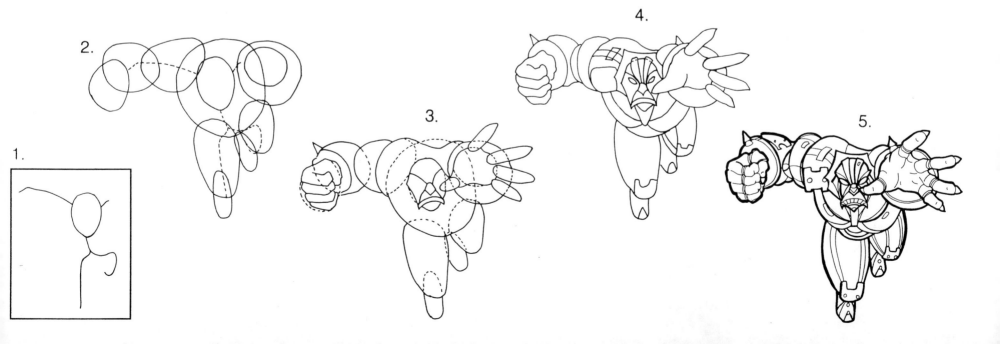

1.   2.   3.   4.   5.

# BUSTER THE BAD

3. Start defining and shaping the muscles within the oval guidelines, erasing your gesture lines as you go along. Then, begin outlining this supervillain's hair, hands, and face.

1.& 2. Starting with the head, draw the simple stick figure (gesture lines). Then add the various overlapping ovals and other guideline shapes.

Use foreshortening when any part of the body points away from you, the viewer. This gives your figure a dramatic, 3-dimensional look.

**Note:** Keep all your guidelines lightly drawn. They will be easier to erase later on.

4. Complete the hair and facial features. Sharply define the hands, and Buster's arm and leg muscles. Then, begin adding the rings on his limbs and other details.

Any unnecessary guidelines should be erased before going to step #5.

5. Now add all the final details and finishing touches, and Buster is ready to be bad!

# DARK DEMON

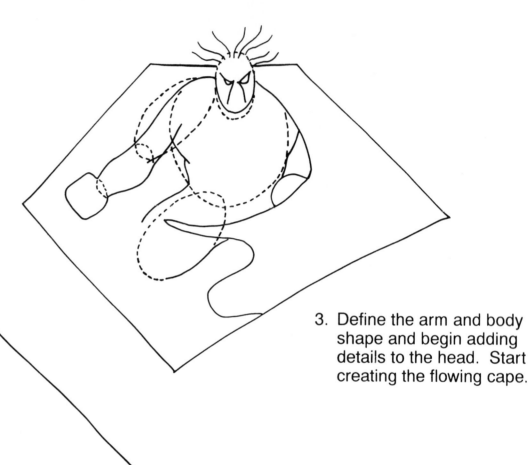

1.& 2. Begin by lightly drawing the basic line figure. Then add the ovals for the body parts and the surrounding straight lines for the cape.

3. Define the arm and body shape and begin adding details to the head. Start creating the flowing cape.

It's easy to draw almost anything if you first build a good foundation.

4. Draw the fingers and blend the body shapes together as you add the clothes. Add the rest of the facial features and complete the cape's outline. Begin adding details.

5. Add all the final details and shading to his face, hair, and clothes. Use a felt-tip pen to complete this super-villain. A heavy outline always adds a dramatic effect to your drawing. Don't forget to attach the arrowheads.

**Note:** Since most villains are sourpusses, their mouths curve downwards.

# GRETA, THE GHASTLY GIANT

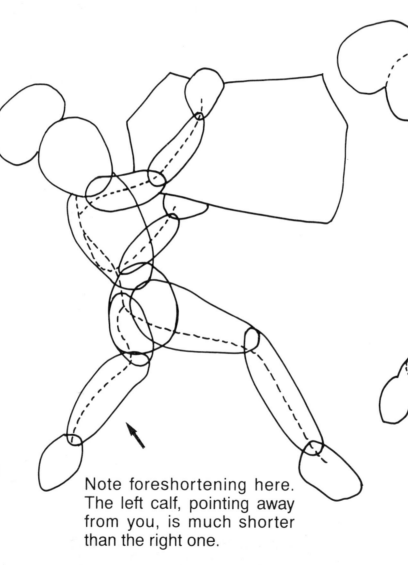

**1.& 2.** Begin this supervillain with the lightly drawn stick figure. Then draw the oval guidelines for the body outline and the outline of the house.

**Note:** Draw these key steps carefully. Get the stick figure to gesture in the directions you want it to. By carefully adding the ovals over the stick figure, you have created a solid foundation. This will give your figure a more realistic look after you've completed the next steps.

Note foreshortening here. The left calf, pointing away from you, is much shorter than the right one.

**3.** Define the body sections within the oval outlines, erasing the stick figure and other guidelines you no longer need.

Add guidelines for her vest and begin shaping the house.

5. Add all the final details and finishing touches as shown. Now Greta can complete her super-villainous mission.

4. Curve and blend all the parts together into a smooth body shape. Add guidelines for the boots, ball and chain, and clothes.

Continue adding wrecking lines to the house.

**Note:** If you're not satisfied with any part of your drawing, erase and start again.

# TORMENT-O-RATOR

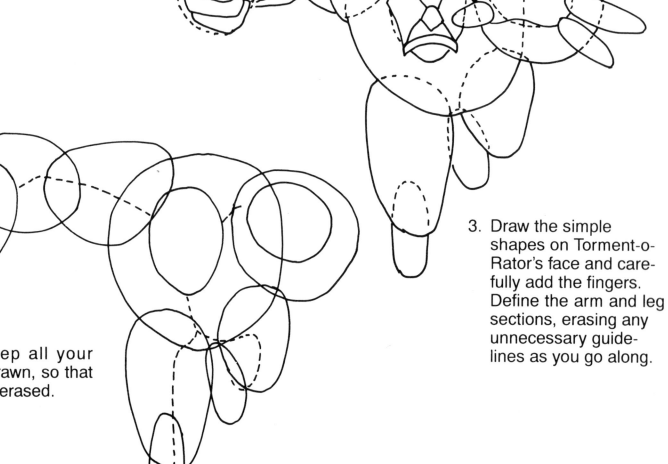

1.& 2. Draw the oval for the
head and the gesture
lines. Then add all the
overlapping ovals for
the arms, legs, and torso.

Remember to keep all your
guidelines lightly drawn, so that
they may be easily erased.

3. Draw the simple
shapes on Torment-o-
Rator's face and care-
fully add the fingers.
Define the arm and leg
sections, erasing any
unnecessary guide-
lines as you go along.

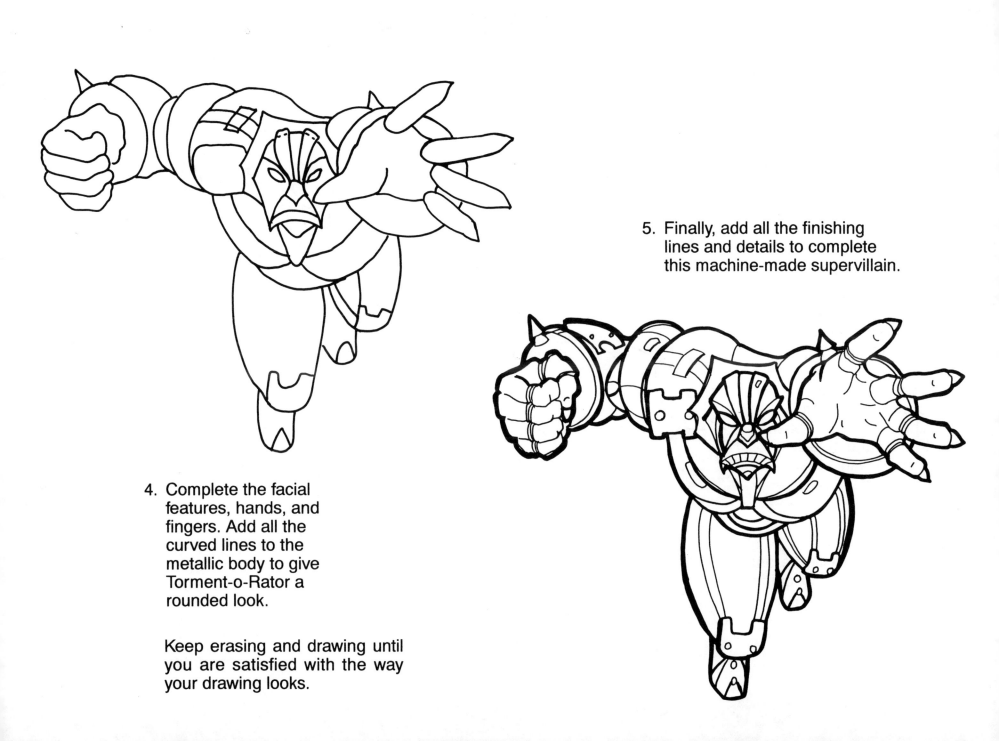

5. Finally, add all the finishing lines and details to complete this machine-made supervillain.

4. Complete the facial features, hands, and fingers. Add all the curved lines to the metallic body to give Torment-o-Rator a rounded look.

Keep erasing and drawing until you are satisfied with the way your drawing looks.

# LITTLE LIONEL

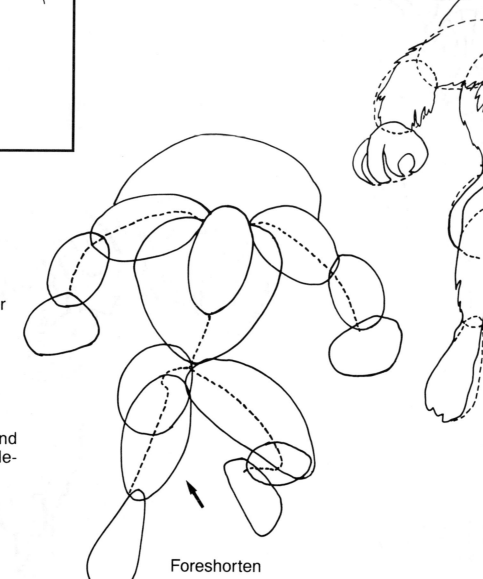

1.& 2. Draw the basic stick
figure and all the
oval body guide-
lines. Note that the
ovals are different
shapes and sizes.
Draw them carefully.
This will make it easier
to draw the muscle
shapes within them.

Erase the stick figure and
other unnecessary guide-
lines as you go along.

Foreshorten

3.  Draw all the body
shapes within the oval
guidelines, carefully
creating Lionel's lion-
like facial features,
claw-like fingers, and
hairy outline.

4. Blend and smooth all the shapes together. Add the bushy mane and finish shaping the face.

5. Complete Little Lionel by adding fangs and claws, and all the other details.

# THE PIT BULLY

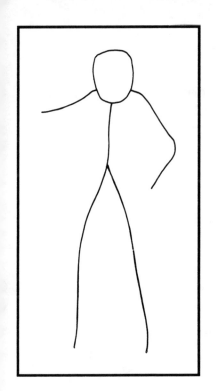

1.& 2. Draw the standing line figure and the oval guideline body shapes. Add guidelines for the cape.

Make sure your figure is gesturing in the direction you want it to before continuing to step 3.

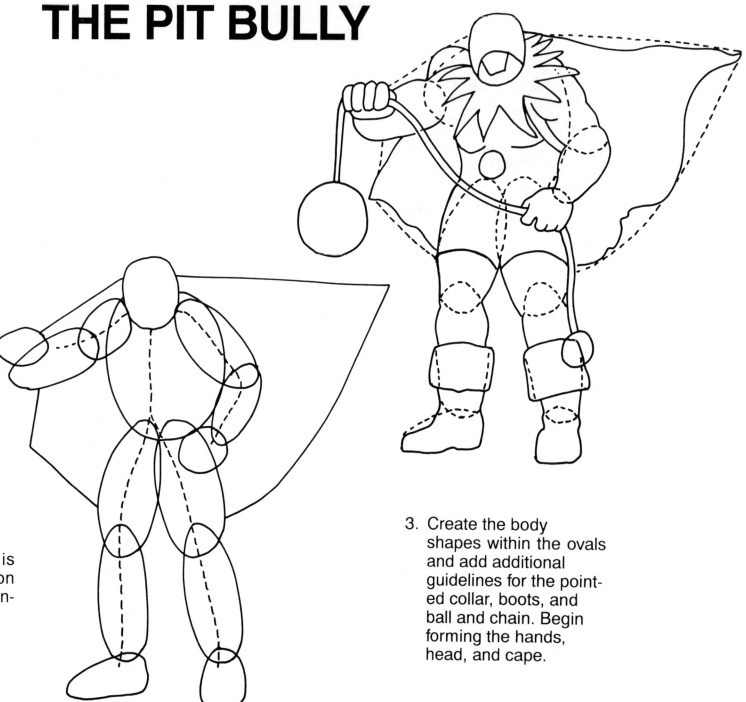

3. Create the body shapes within the ovals and add additional guidelines for the pointed collar, boots, and ball and chain. Begin forming the hands, head, and cape.

4. Blend Pit Bully's body parts together and finish drawing his hands. Begin adding details to the clothes, head, and ball and chain. Complete the cape.

Erase any guidelines you no longer need and when you're satisfied with the way your drawing looks, start adding the finishing touches.

5. Add all the final details and shading to complete this supervillain. Now your personal Pit Bully is ready for some hair-raising havoc!

**Note:** Supervillains have abnormally large muscle lines that make them appear powerful and dangerous.

# THE VAPORIZER

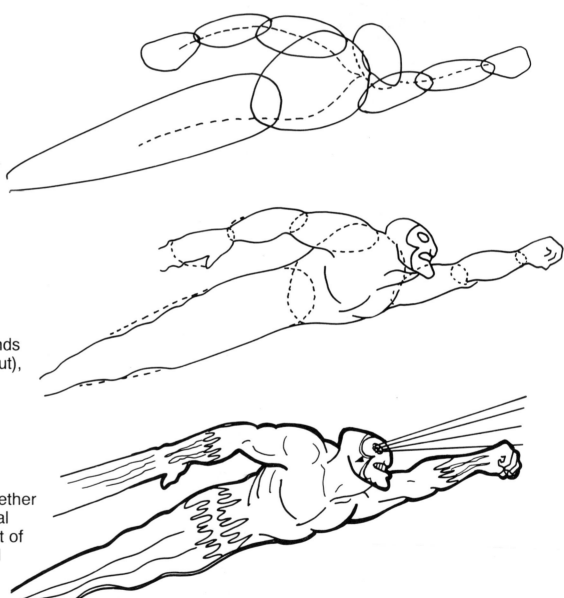

1.& 2. Draw the basic stick figure and all the overlapping oval body guidelines.

Make sure you have built a solid foundation with the first two steps before continuing.

3. Sketch the body parts within the oval guidelines. Begin forming the Vaporizer's hands and facial features (note how his chin juts out), erasing guidelines as you go along.

4. Blend the arm, shoulder, and chest muscles together into a smooth upper body shape. Finish the facial features and add the vaporizing lines coming out of his eye. Extend the flowing body and right-hand lines, and add the final details.

Tear On Perforated Line

# THE MEANY GENIE

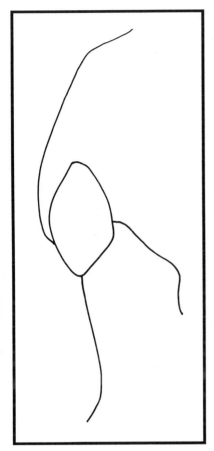

3. Draw the big arm muscles within the guidelines. Then create the hands, fingers, lamp, and basic facial features.

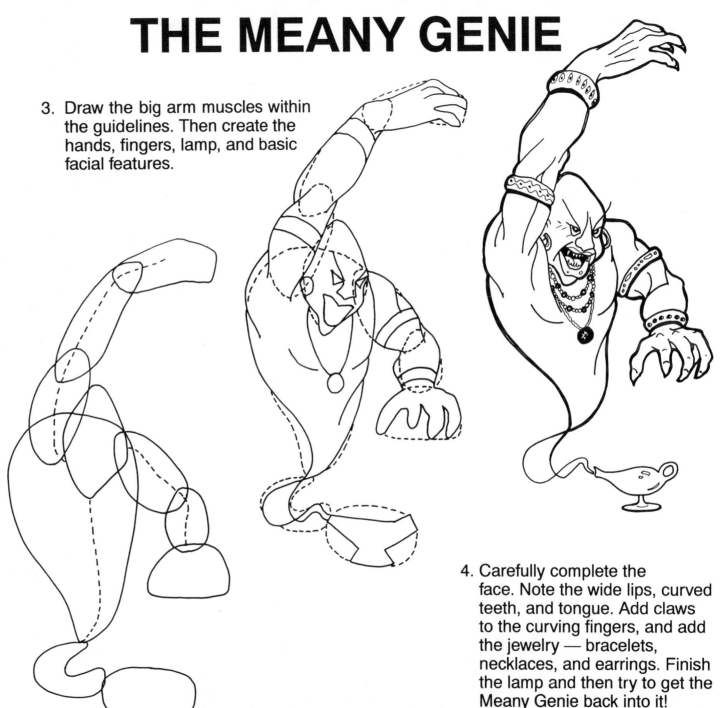

1.& 2. Starting with the head, draw the gesturing stick figure. Add the broad upper body and arm guidelines, and the shape for the magic lamp.

Erase any guidelines you no longer need.

4. Carefully complete the face. Note the wide lips, curved teeth, and tongue. Add claws to the curving fingers, and add the jewelry — bracelets, necklaces, and earrings. Finish the lamp and then try to get the Meany Genie back into it!

# RATSY RIZZI

3. Create all the parts of Ratsy's body within the guideline shapes. Add guidelines for her facial features, mask, and gloves.

1.& 2. Starting with the oval-shaped head, draw the basic stick figure. Add the broad body ovals and shapes for the hands, feet, and ears.

Pay special attention to the overlapping ovals on the upper left leg. This is another example of foreshortening. Your eyes are fooled and don't see the full length of the leg. Draw it the way it **looks** and not how it really is. Remember to keep these guidelines lightly drawn.

4. Finish the facial features, mask, and gloves. Begin adding the tail. Blend all the shapes into a smooth outline, erasing any lines you no longer need as you go along.

5. Complete the tail and add all the finishing touches. Don't forget Ratsy's whiskers. Use your imagination when adding details. Draw a different mask or clothes if you wish. Or, create a scene with several supervillains in it.

# GRAFFITI GUS

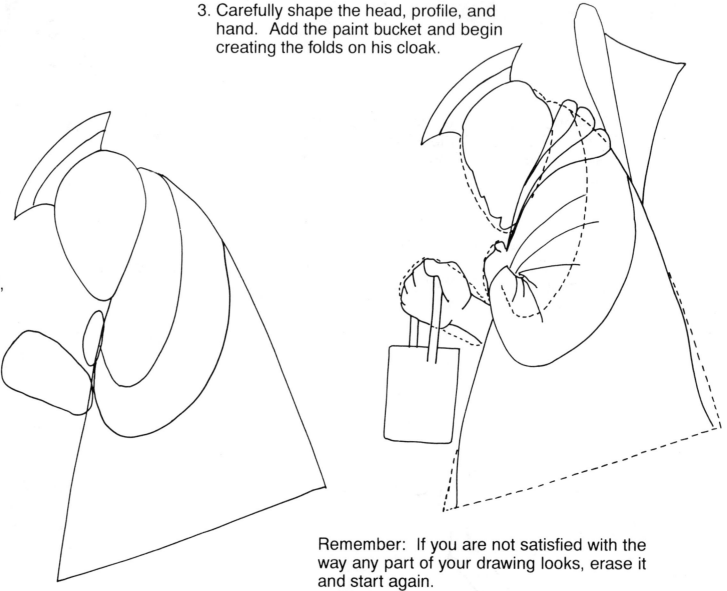

3. Carefully shape the head, profile, and hand. Add the paint bucket and begin creating the folds on his cloak.

1.& 2. Starting with a large oval shape for the head, create the basic figure, drawing the additional shapes as shown.

Remember: If you are not satisfied with the way any part of your drawing looks, erase it and start again.

Erase any guidelines that are no longer needed.

5. Now complete your drawing by adding lots of details and shading. For the finishing touches, add some of Gus's favorite graffiti.

4. Finish the face and hair, and add the brushes and dripping paint. Complete the supervillain's flowing cloak.

# MAGNET-O-MAN

3. Within the ovals, create the basic body parts, erasing the stick figure as you go along. Carefully add guidelines for his magnetized chest shield, belt, and knee guards.

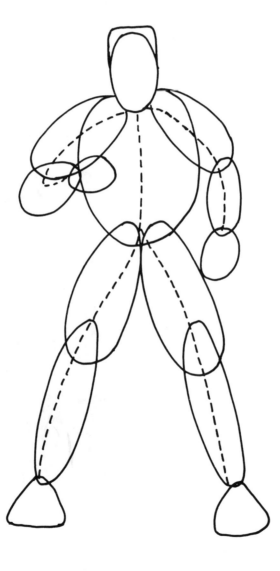

1. & 2. Lightly draw the standing stick figure and all the oval guideline shapes around it.

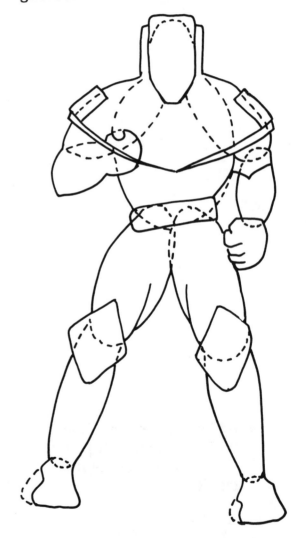

4. Blend and shape all the forms together, paying close attention to how all the shapes and lines interconnect. Start adding the facial features, hood, boots, magneto spear, and other details.

5. Add lots more details to complete Magnet-O-Man. Note how the use of heavy lines gives the final drawing a dramatic look.

Keep erasing and drawing until you're completely satisfied with your work. Remember, practice makes perfect.

# HULKOID, THE WILD BIKER

Remember to keep all your guidelines lightly drawn.

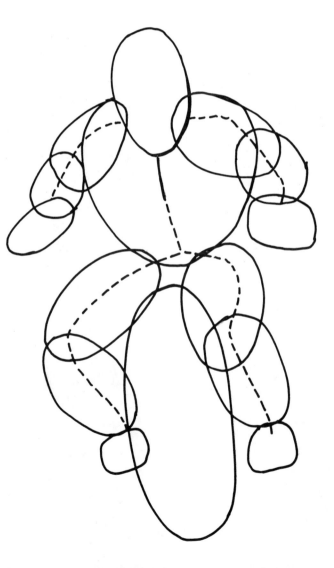

1.& 2. Make sure the legs of the guideline stick figure are spread far apart to allow for the powerful leg muscles and bike. Then add the large oval shapes for the body and tire.

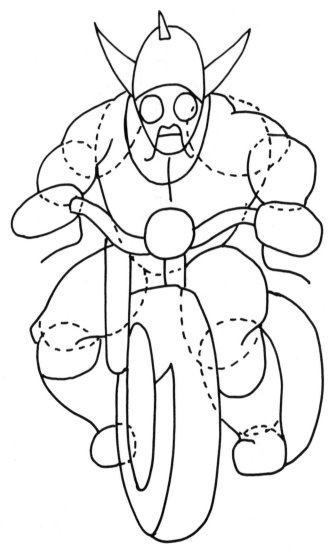

3. Draw the basic body shapes within the ovals and start outlining the face, helmet, fingers, and boots. Note the foreshortened arms. Add the handlebars and other parts of the bike.

5. Add the finishing touches to this wild biker by completing all the details. Add heavy shading to his helmet, gloves, and boots. When you're done, outline the rest of Hulkoid's body with a felt-tip pen.

4. Erase unnecessary guidelines as you blend the shapes together. Carefully curve all the body lines as you define the muscles. Then start adding details to Hulkoid's face, body, and bike.

# BAD-MAGIC MARVIN

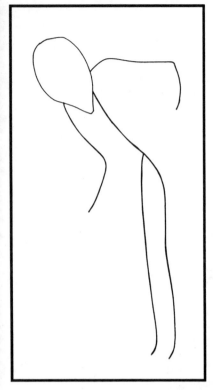

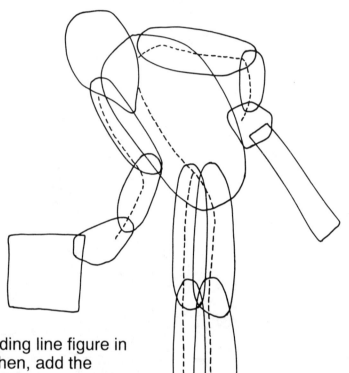

1.& 2. Draw the simple, standing line figure in the pose as shown. Then, add the various oval body shapes. Note the rectangular guidelines for Marvin's hat and cane.

3. Sketch the body parts within the oval guidelines, erasing the stick figure as you go along. Begin forming the hands and facial features, and create guidelines for his jacket, ruffles, and flowing hair.

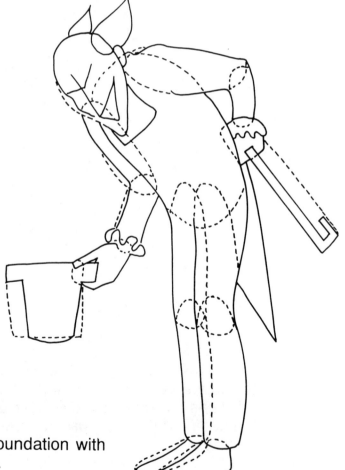

Make sure you have built a solid foundation with the first two steps before continuing.

4. Blend the body shapes together and complete the face, vest, jacket, hat, and cane.

If you're not satisfied with the way any part of your drawing looks, erase it and start again.

5. Finish Mad Marvin's clothes and face, and add all the final details so this supervillain can make his ghostly friend disappear.

# VILLAINELLA

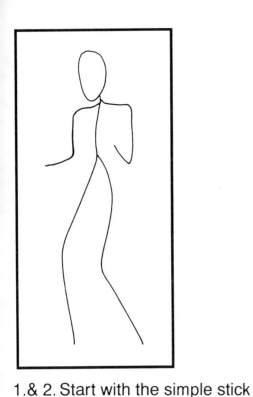

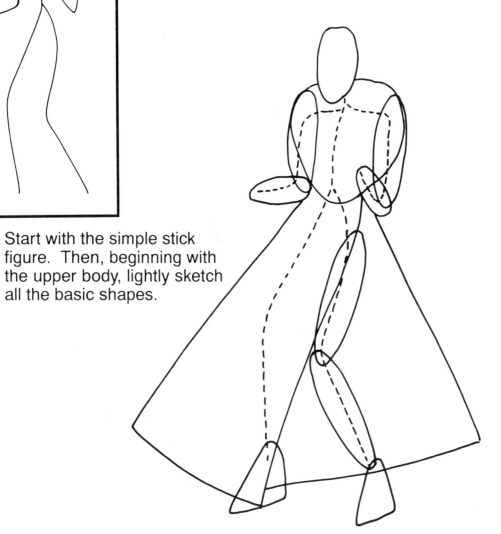

1.& 2. Start with the simple stick figure. Then, beginning with the upper body, lightly sketch all the basic shapes.

3. Draw guidelines for her hands, hair, facial features, and cape. Begin forming her skirt and leg, as shown. Remember to erase any unnecessary lines as you continue to refine your drawing.

4. Blend the guidelines together, and finish the face and hair. Note the curved mouth. Complete the fingers, clothes, and cape, and start adding details.

5. Continue adding details to the clothes as you continue to refine your drawing. Keep erasing and sketching until you're satisfied with the way Villainella looks. Use a thick marker to give her hair a dramatic look.

# THE EVIL ROBO BAT

1. & 2. Lightly draw the stick figure and all the guideline shapes around it. This super-villain has huge wings, so draw your lines accordingly.

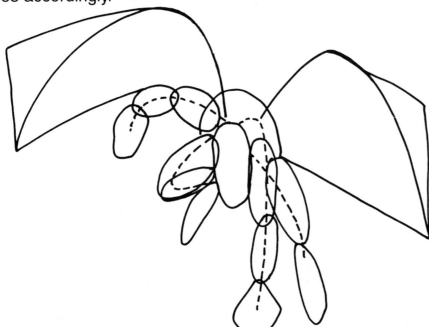

3. First, lightly sketch the body parts within the oval shapes, paying careful attention to the hands, feet, and wings. Next, start creating the head, erasing any lines you no longer need.

4. Complete the head and wings. Some of the parts of Robo Bat's body **don't** blend together, they butt into each other. Note how the tips of his wings curl to match his fangs and fingers.

5. For the finishing touches, add lots of lines all over the bat's body, face, and wings, giving him a real "robo" appearance.

These are just a few of the weapons
that you can add to any of your super-villainous drawings.
Use your imagination and create many more.

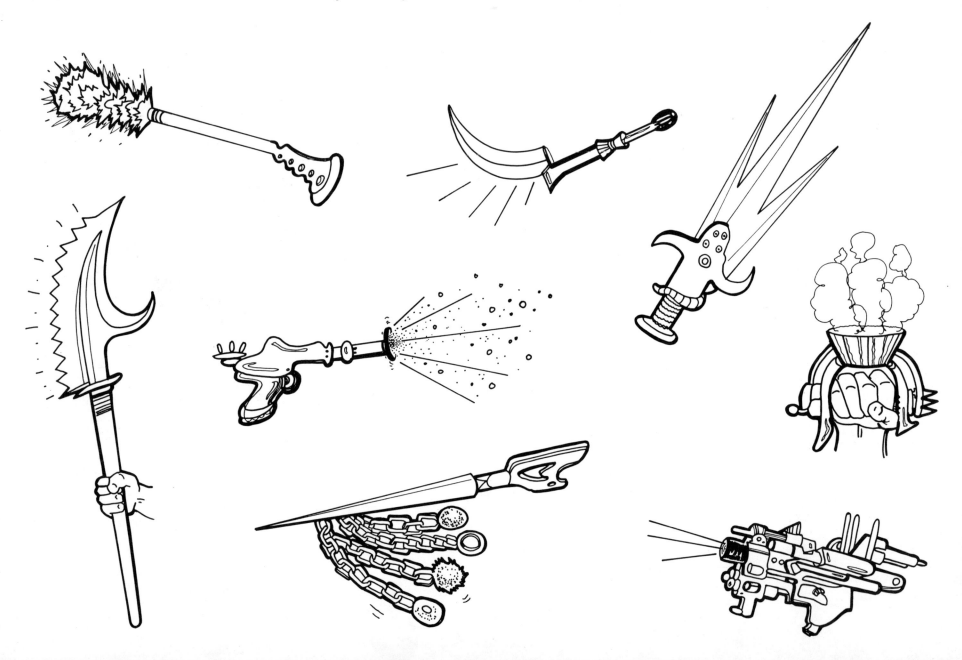